COMMUNION OF LIFE

COMMUNION

Meditations for

Westminster John Knox Press
Louisville, Kentucky

OF LIFE

the New Millennium

Grateful acknowledgment is made for permission to reproduce photographs from the National Geographic Image Collection. Photo credits are listed by days: 1, 5, 11, 14, 17, 26, 38, 44, Raymond Gehman; 2, 4, 39, 48, Medford Taylor; 3, 9, 15, 32, 37, 41, Bruce Dale; 6, 31, Todd Gipstein; 7, 12, Jonathan Blair; 8, 23, 24, 35, Chris Johns; 10, James Stanfield; 13, 25, Philip Schermeister; 16, 47, William Allard; 18, 20, Maria Stenzel; 19, 22, 30, 42, Richard Olsenius; 21, 40, 45, James Blair; 27, David Harvey; 28, 29, Thad Samuels Abell II; 33, Gilbert M. Grosvenor; 34, Joel Sartore; 36, Joseph Scherschel; 43, Barry Bishop; 46, Randy Olson.

Book design by Jennifer K. Cox and Dean Nicklas

First edition

Published by Westminster John Knox Press
Louisville, Kentucky

PRINTED IN SINGAPORE

99 00 01 02 03 04 05 06 07 08 — 10 9 8 7 6 5 4 3 2 1

Library of Congress Cataloging-in-Publication Data
Glaser, Chris.
    Communion of life : meditations for the new millennium / by
Chris Glaser. — 1st ed.
       p.   cm.
    ISBN 0-664-22127-0 (alk. paper)
    1. Meditations.   I. Title.
BL624.2.G57   1999
291.4'32—dc21   98-47597

Wondrous me—
Earth, air, water, fire.
Wondrous you—
Earth, air, water, fire.
Collaborators of existence,
Communion of life.

To those on a spiritual quest—
In thanksgiving for all that is sacred.

Preface

What is the "communion of life"? Every spiritual path has offered a slightly different answer to that question, and that's as it should be. Every people and culture has a different perspective on life and its meaning. Instead of viewing the variety of spiritual paths as competitive or mutually exclusive, it is far more practical, realistic, and vital to recognize that the whole is more complete, that each path has something to offer those on a spiritual quest—that is, those looking for the luminous essence of things that illumines our way, enlightens our mind, and impassions our heart.

I use the metaphor Communion of Life to mean that way in which we realize our connectedness with one another, with the universe, with the sacred. Some may do this within religion; others may wish to avoid the trappings of religion. Many people have no religious background. Others may have experienced religious environments that were spiritually abusive, denying their sacred worth; or spiritually confining and controlling, limiting their spiritual quest. Yet, in truth, spirituality enhances life and spills past boundaries. Religious or not, we are all spiritual people who may choose to discover, discern, develop, deepen, and expand our spirituality. These meditations are intended for all who are on such a quest.

Along with present day teachers such as Joseph Campbell and Thomas Moore, I believe that the spiritual quest needs imagination, creativity, and mythology. There has been a modern emphasis on the *practical* results of religion and spirituality, especially in the United States—to induce morality, justice, inner peace, and prosperity. We often have little patience for the "impractical" in religion, "wasting" time in contemplation of life's mystery. There has even been a movement to "demythologize" our faiths in favor of a rationalistic worldview. While these serve as helpful corrections to navel-gazing and to literalistic interpretations of sacred texts and stories, I believe that such efforts cause us to lose much of the enchantment, pleasure, beauty, imagination, and play inherent in mythology. Without the metaphors of myth, it's difficult (if not impossible) to think, speak, and dialogue about the invisible qualities that make life more than what we see, smell, hear, sense, taste, even think and feel. In a sense, we need to *re-mythologize* our culture to discover sacred awe and wonder. Ironically (since science and religion are purportedly opposed to one another), science may help us do that in the new millennium as we are faced with greater and greater mysteries of the universe and of life itself.

Science has its own mythology, and this book will utilize one of its earliest mythological frameworks. The ancients believed that earth, air, water, and fire were the four elements of all existence—that these companions, in various relationships, provided the Communion of Life. Using this mythological premise, I hope these meditations will guide you toward an understanding and experience of spirituality as a here-and-now rather than an other-worldly or by-and-by encounter with the holy, the cosmic, the divine. Natural elements may reveal the supernatural. Thus our spirituality may remain grounded and embodied in "ordinary" experience, which itself becomes extraordinary and sacred in contemplation. The cyclical repetition of the themes of earth, air, water, and fire also link us to "natural time"—that is, time which parallels the cycle of life and seasons of nature rather than time measured mechanistically by a clock.

Poetry may be the language and scripture of the "secular" mystic. Of course, there is no such thing as a secular mystic, but I use this phrase to suggest those who seek the holy outside the parameters of organized religion. These meditations became poetic in their writing. Both poetry and meditation anticipate the thoughtful pause—the attentiveness needed in the spiritual life. The reader may be tempted to read through these pages quickly, possibly in one sitting.

Yet, unlike much other reading material, the meditations that follow are not intended for *information*, but *illumination*. As with all readings for the spirit, they serve better when taken one day or one reflection period at a time, reading slowly, possibly aloud, breathing deeply, allowing the words, a phrase at a time, to descend with the mind into the heart in a quiet state of rest, thus enabling feelings and thoughts to brew within the depths of the soul and emerge as aromas of a slowly cooked spiritual feast. A single phrase may become your mantra for your meditation or your day.

No single volume of meditations is sufficient to lead one into a fully developed spirituality. That is a lifelong quest, and requires the assistance of a host of spiritual guides. This book may simply serve to awaken or enhance your spiritual quest, and that is my hope.

Chris Glaser
Atlanta, Georgia

Acknowledgments

Stephanie Egnotovich, executive editor at Westminster John Knox Press, suggested to me writing a book for those seeking spirituality outside the parameters of religion. She had noticed a fellow airplane passenger reading such a book and initiated a conversation about his choice of reading material. He explained that he had no religious background and was attempting to discover spirituality.

I am grateful for Stephanie's suggestion. It struck a familiar chord in my own experience, because part of my work has been to assist those with no religious heritage or an abusive religious upbringing to discover spirituality as a good and vital and necessary perspective on life. I believe everyone has a spirituality, a way in which they "put things together" and make sense of the world, a faith that prompts them to get out of bed in the morning. The spiritual quest is often discerning the core of such spirituality, intentionally cultivating and developing it, as well as correcting and expanding it with the input of those one recognizes as spiritual authorities and with the support of a chosen spiritual community.

I am grateful for Stephanie's fellow traveler, too, for as I wrote these meditations I kept him in mind, perhaps someday reading them on a plane in the midst of a busy life.

My background has been largely in religion, but I have found religion often caught up in tedious and trivial debates, less able to remind me of the awesome nature of life and the cosmos. The revelations of science have often come to my rescue, reminding me of our amazing world and our amazing selves. Science awakens my sense that there's more to life than meets the eye. Science has expanded my spirituality. Thus I am grateful for the way in which science has helped inspire these meditations. I am especially grateful for one scientist who served as a reader of my manuscript, offering helpful corrections—my friend Brian Davison, Ph.D., a biochemical engineer in Knoxville, Tennessee.

As always, I thank the good folk at Westminster John Knox Press who have copyedited and proofed this book, and will publicize, market, and distribute it. I thank Stephanie Egnotovich for editorial recommendations and for selecting the best visual images to accompany the text. I thank Jennifer Cox and Dean Nicklas for their superb work designing this book. I thank the National Geographic Society, whose photographers provided those images, for keeping people's wonder alive in its work.

I thank also the unsung heroes of publishing, the book distributors and booksellers who assist writers and readers in finding one another. And finally, as always, I thank you, the reader, for sharing my interest in the spiritual quest.

Chris Glaser

Sacred earth:
Holding us fast,
Whirling to keep us steady,
Shifting axis to temper climate,
Yielding nutrients for life.

Holy ground:
A grassy belly cradling us in rest,
A rounded, rocky bosom inspiring dreamers,
A birth canal whose current is destiny.

Grateful, grateful am I,
To stand, to sit, to lie on you,
To ride, to sail, to drive on you,
To look down, to look up, to look out
And see you there.

Sacred ground,
I remove my shoes in reverence.

CYCLE ONE

Blessed air:
Caressing and cooling.
A hot, dry blast.
Chilling to the bone.
Lifting up, holding up.
Trying to knock me to the ground.

You touch me in your varied expressions
And offer survival in all of them.
I am thankful.
In you I live and move and have my being,
Yet, when you are silent and still,
I seldom notice you, unless
You bring pollen or pollution,
Or scents of flower, flavor, or lover.

Without you is vacuum:
Empty, suffocating, devoid of life—
At least, life as I know it.
I take you into myself,
I am filled with you,
I release you unto thyself,
All with thanksgiving.

Holy water:

Condensed in cumulus clouds.

Ubiquitous as damp fog or steamy humidity.

Spitting, dripping, pouring from the sky.

Cleansing, quenching, feeding, flooding earth.

Flaking, drifting, covering, brightening earth.

Hardening, icing, pounding, tearing earth.

Falling, melting, flowing down streams and rivers.

Gurgling over smooth stones, shooting over precipices.

Filling ponds and lakes and oceans and us

With your moist, sweet and salty kisses.

Keep to your boundaries, and I welcome you.

You are welcome.

Christen me afresh.

Hallowed fire,
Visibly and invisibly you glow
Outside and inside, flagrant and hidden,
From sun to moon to stars
To leaves to creatures to dreams—
A chemical metamorphosis that creates and sustains life,
A spark, an ember, a candle,
A hearth, a campfire, a furnace,
A flame, a fire, an inferno—
purifying, warming, illuminating,
burning, destroying, rampaging.

Awed by the fire that gives life,
We fear the fire that brings death.
We are in awe,
We are in fear,
We are in hope
Of fire.
Kindle my spirit, sacred fire.

You offer security.
You are solid under me.
I walk,
And you seem to glide beneath my feet,
Catching my footsteps,
Preventing a fall into the abyss.

True, at times, you seem too fixed,
Unmoved, unresponsive, unyielding.
Then you hurt, aggravate, block.
That's your nature.
My faith does not want to move your mountains—
But rather, aspire to their triumph
Touching the sky.

When you do move beneath us—
Quaking, sliding, collapsing—
Our safety vanishes.
We need you to be invincible, for
The earth in us is so vulnerable.

You wave our flags,
Float our balloons,
Carry our kites,
Fly our planes,
Power our windmills,
Freshen our homes,
Ventilate our factories:

We think it's us,
When, in truth, it's you.
We've simply got wind of you—
Your essence.
If our wind was knocked out of us,
Life would expire.
Air.

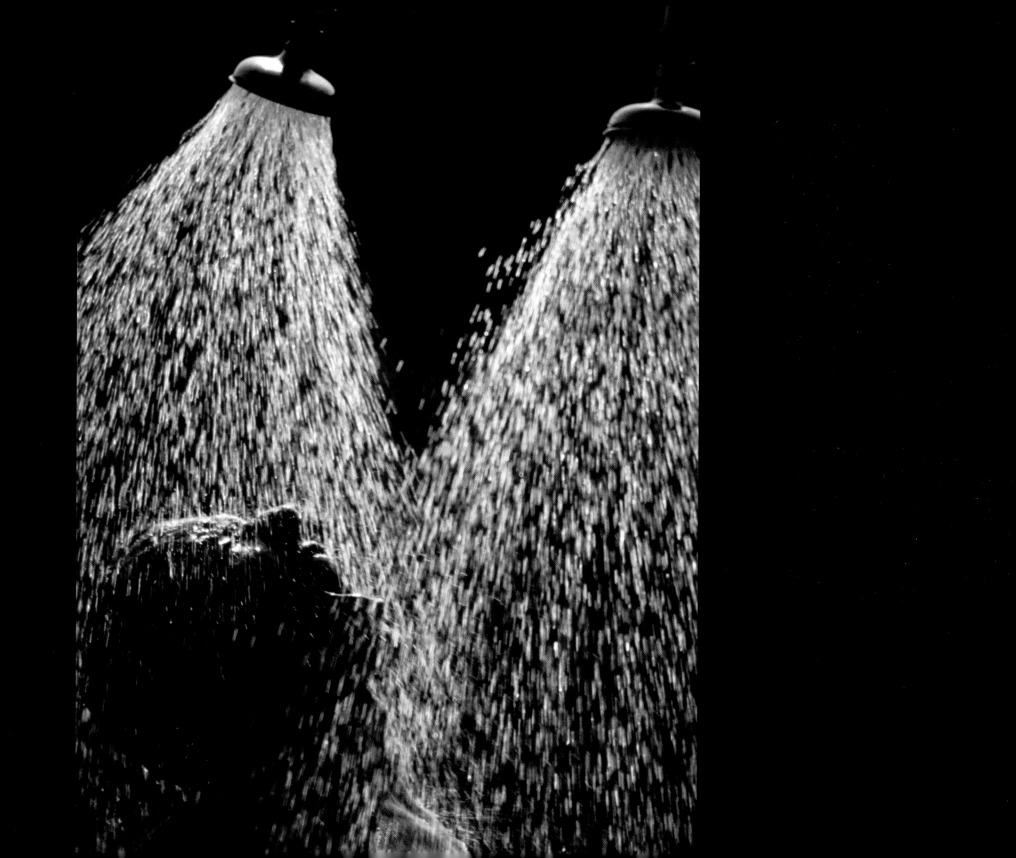

You live within me—
In my eyes, in my flesh,
In my thoughts, in my movements:
My liquidity.

You cleanse me inside and out,
Rinsing each cell,
Flushing out toxins,
Boiling out sweat,
Crying out grief.

Most of me is you.
Before air, I knew you,
Bundled by embryonic fluids:
Echo of primordial waters
Where first were fused
Earth, air, water, fire,
The things that make for life.

As you held me,
Now I hold you,
Precious, unasked gift from eternity—
Living water.

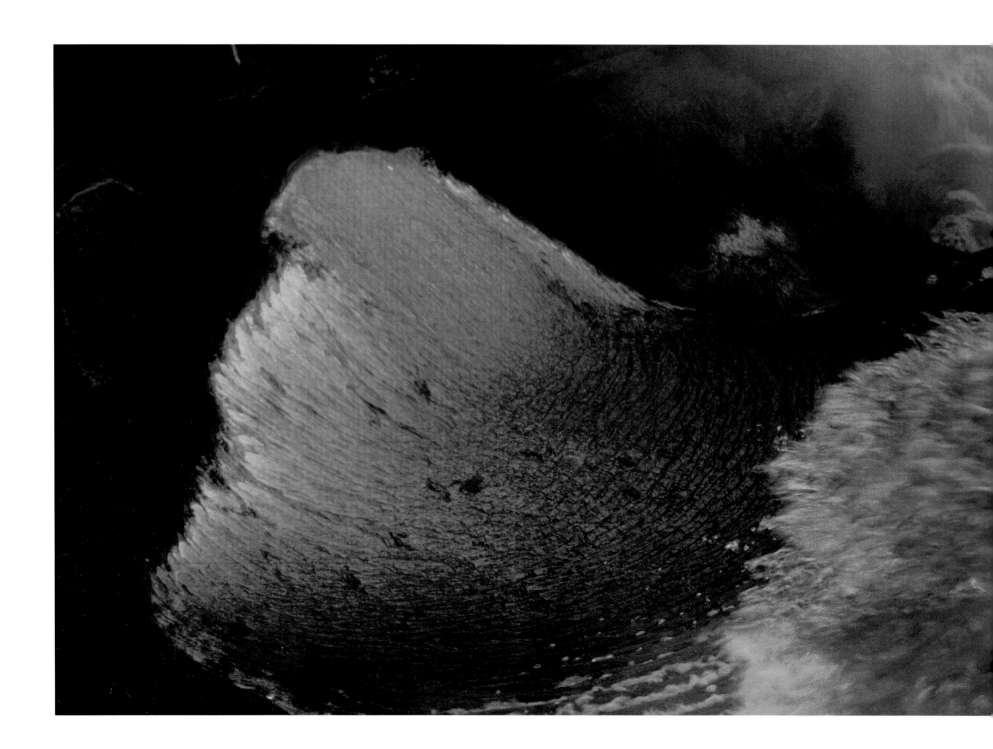

You demand our attention.
You insist. You compel.
From the warning, "Fire!"
To a match struck in a black cavern,
Unveiling natural art deep in earth;
From a spark of understanding in a child's eye
To the dawn of an unlived day.

You awaken our senses, our wonder, our reverence,
Quicken our spirits, enlighten our minds,
Reveal shadows of fear and of doubt.
Obsessed insects burn in your glory,
Healthy seeds grow toward your light.

We bask in your warmth,
View color invoked by your reflection,
Feed on life glowing with your energy,
Hide in silhouettes cut from your radiance.
And still, unconsumed and unconcerned,
You burn.

angible earth,

You touch yourself through us.

We grasp your hand,

Stroke your fur,

Prune your branches,

Cast your stones,

Bury your seed,

Birth your children.

But it's not just us,

It's you in us.

You have developed your sense of touch

Within our bodies—

Communing through us

With air, water, fire,

In pleasure, buoyancy, and passion;

And communing through us with yourself

Delightedly, painfully, compassionately:

A communion of life

Giving rise to soul:

More than the sum of your parts.

Earth—in us, in me,

You have become sensual and sensitive.

Blessed earth!

The sun's glory
Wraps around us,
Dives into valleys,
Peaks behind ridges,
Slinks through city streets,
Explodes on beaches,
As if through thin air.

The sun's grandeur
Glows green through branches,
Bounces lavender off irises,
Mushrooms grey above factories,
Canopies blue on clear days,
Gilds with age,
As if through thin air.

The sun's gospel
Proclaimed to earth's ends
Effortlessly, gracefully,
Baptizing us all,
Just and unjust,
Believer and nonbeliever,
Grateful and ungrateful,
Enlightened and unenlightened—
Immersing us all
In our star's splashing splendor
As if through thin air.

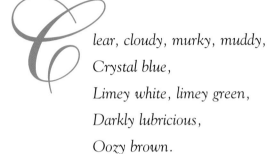lear, cloudy, murky, muddy,
Crystal blue,
Limey white, limey green,
Darkly lubricious,
Oozy brown.

Yet there's more to you when arched across the sky—
Lavender, blue, green, yellow, orange, red—
A Ninja warrior
Visible or invisible at will,
A will not your own,
But touched or grasped or moved—
Mystically transformed by compañeros:
Earth, air, the fire of the sun.

*U*nseen, you

Warm the room,

Bake the bread,

Spark the car,

Illuminate the world;

Drive the machines,

Play the toys,

Sing the stereo,

Televise the world;

Sound the alarm,

Preserve the food,

Record the message,

Communicate the world.

Wire fire:

Spark of imagination

Invisibly kindled

By falling water,

By force of steam,

By wafting air

Turning blades of once molten earth

Dynamically;

Hurling fire farther than any volcano

Discretely;

Sustaining fire in numerous venues

Remotely.

Hidden power,

Metaphoria,

Spīritus.

Our original sin
Is not the seizing of forbidden fruit,
But failing to see
The infinite in the finite,
The luminous, sacred essence
Of the garden;

Failing to revere
The life that gives us life;
Trampling on the taboo,
Sequestering, quantifying,
And qualifying the holy—
The heart of our garden.

Forgive us, earth,
Be merciful in our willful ignorance
As you are gracious in your altruistic nature.
Hold us accountable, and then,
Hold us.

Whooshing,

Rustling,

Purring,

Silencing,

We're listening:

Speak.

Vibrating,

Echoing,

Exhaling,

Inhaling,

We're listening:

Speak.

Bubbling,

Fizzing,

Slamming,

Popping,

We're listening:

Speak.

Jars,
  Tidepools,
Pipes,
   Geysers,
Gutters,
   Shores,
Aqueducts,
   Banks,
Canals,
   Deltas,
Dikes,
   Cliffs,
Dams,
   Ridges—

Yet you escape!
   Evaporating,
Overflowing,
   Overwhelming,
Bursting—
   Thirsty for camaraderie:
Uplifted in air;
Bonding with earth;
Stimulated by fire:
Elemental communion,
   Simple and sacred,
Miracle au naturel.

Heart,

    Hearth,

Sentiment,

Kindling feelings of belonging—

Home, family, faith, friend, country, earth.

We burn inside,

Warming at hope,

Glowing in love,

Sparking in joy,

Stinging in grief,

Searing in anger,

Exploding in passion,

Imploding in abandonment.

We tend our fires,

Keep them burning,

Until they burn up or out.

If up, to where?

If out, of what?

Energy's not lost,

But transformed:

Yet how?

To what?

Stones—

Nestled in a riverbed;

Character of a landscape;

Ringed around a garden;

Lined along a path.

Stones—

Chroniclers of geologic time;

Placed to plot the planets;

Arranged to greet the seasons;

Markers of our passings.

Stones—

Laid down for a foundation;

Stacked to make a wall;

Built into a structure;

Clustered for a cloister.

Stones—

Spewn from a volcano;

Tumbling down a mountain;

Hurtling through space;

Colliding with air for fire.

Stones—

Flashing through sky.

Down to earth.

Stones.

CYCLE FIVE

You love us well;
You seek us out,
You long to fill our vacuums,
You love to feed our lungs.

Breezily, you tickle us,
Saucily, you tousle our hair,
Intimately, you touch our inner places,
Lovingly, you embrace us everywhere.

Where on earth may I flee your desire for me?
Where in the cosmos may I escape my need of you?
You blend with my blood to feed and fire my body,
With water, earth, and fire you make your home in me.

Yet you blow where you will,
Mixing with your associates variously,
Homemaking all I touch, smell, see, and hear,
Making me kin to all.

Thy kindom come,
On earth is heaven.

Cleanse me,
Purify me,
Baptize me.

Cleanse me of all that clings to me,
All that is not essential in me,
Whatever holds me from my destiny.

Purify me of contravening intentions,
All that confuses and confounds me,
Whatever counters my holiness.

Baptize me with your flowing grace,
Immersing me in all that is lovely,
Becoming my sacrament of belonging.

Cleanse me,
Purify me,
Baptize me.

Fire me up!
Give me spirit!
Kindle my flame
As fatigue envelops me.

Light my way!
Illumine my mind!
Clarify my vision
As shadows surround me.

Warm me within!
Tend to my heart!
Fuel my compassion
As coldness creeps in.

Six feet of earth
Renders us grave.
Six feet of earth
(More or less)
Renders us life.

We are soil borrowed from earth,
Invested in thought and feeling,
Returned with more or less interest.

The prosperity is the earth's,
The indebtedness is ours,
The transaction is life.

Six feet of earth
(More or less)
Renders us life.
Six feet of earth
Renders us grave.

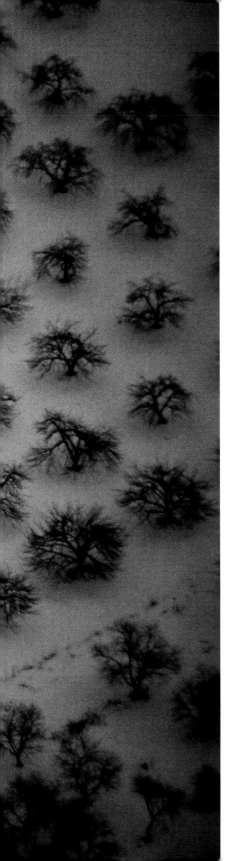

Animator,
Breath of life,
Oxygenator of cells,
Why?

To what end?
To what purpose?
If, if there is a destiny,
What is the origin?
The initial inspiration?
The inaugural aspiration?
The prime inspirator
Or conspirators?

Water, earth, fire, air
And—?
There's more to you than meets the eye.
There's more to you than makes the eye.
Vision calls forth vision.
Ours is partial,
An end rather than the means,
A goal rather than the beginning—
A beginning as invisible
(Or transparent?)
As air.

You come from on high:
From sky to mountaintop,
Peak to ravine,
Ravine to plain,
Plain to shore.

You come from below:
From earth to well,
Well to ground,
Ground to air,
Air to sky.

You come from all sides,
From sea to swell,
Swell to tide,
Tide to wave,
Wave to shore.

You come from within,
From molten core to searing current,
Searing current to hot spring,
Hot spring to heated bodies,
Heated bodies to sweat.

What is the heart
That pulses your liquid
Through earth and air and fire
To renew and refresh us?

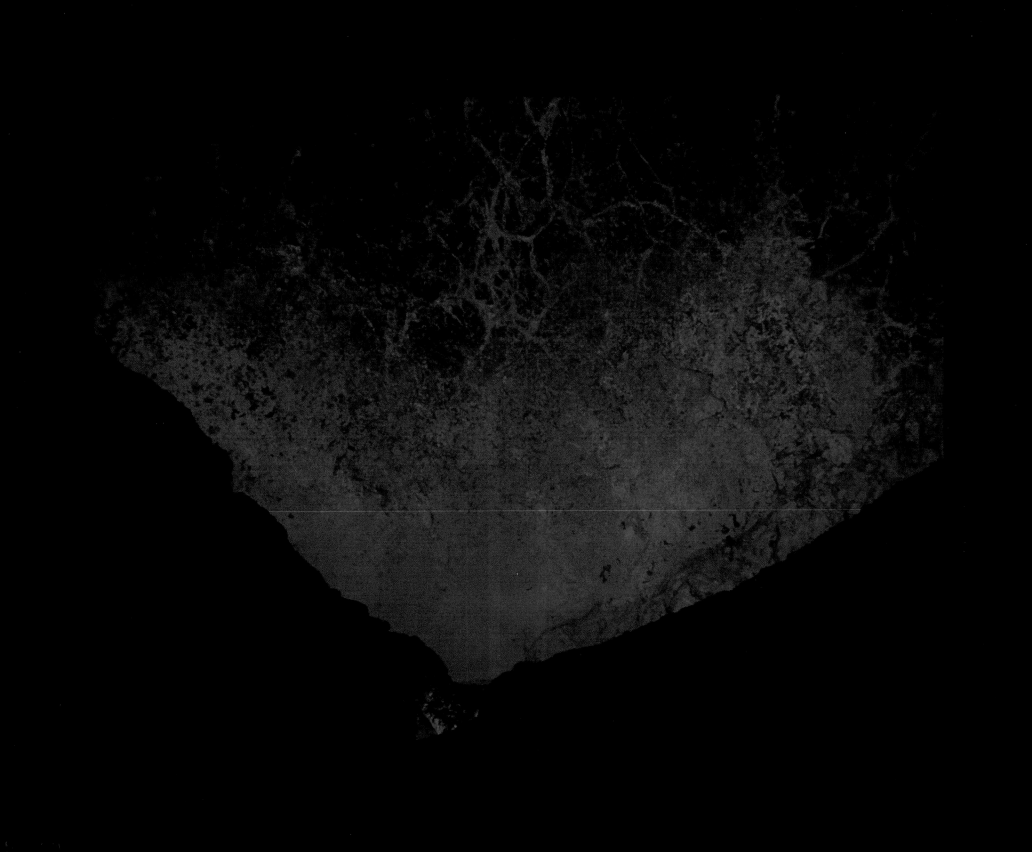

*F*orge of life,

I see you burning in a thousand galaxies,

Churning, yearning, choosing life.

I am here now, in this moment, in this place,

Because of billions of years of your quest:

Blending and baking water and earth and air

Till life appears,

And now, my tiniest part of it.

Was it your idea? Are your only thoughts my own?

Accident? I have little faith in chance.

The spark of life must be sparked to life:

What inspiration? Whose? Why?

The how, as complex as that is, seems more discernible.

And if you choose life for the universe,

And, specifically, narrowly, for me—

For me! For me? For me—

Why do I not absolutely trust your leading?

Death, too, is part of your straining ahead.

Not my choice, but yours,

And you've been doing so well for so much longer

Than I can imagine, than I will continue!

Blessings on you, the fire of life,

Kindled, burning, flashing, dying in me—

A flicker in the world, yet more

Than any thoughtless, unfeeling supernova.

I will let my light shine.

I will let my light shine.

Earth loving earth:
An ancient alchemy
Making earth light as air,
Refreshing as water,
Hot as fire.

Bodies revolving round one another,
Celestial and sensual alike,
Fixed by one another's path,
Drawn by unseen gravity:
A tug of hold or heart or hope.
Though never at the same point at the same time,
Traversing the universe together.

Feeling or fact,
Such force fastens us,
Makes us belong,
Makes us one.

CYCLE SEVEN

Touch me,
Touch me everywhere,
Touch me through every living creature.

I ignore your still touch
As you rest against my face,
Beneath my clothes,
Outside my body,
Waiting to be let in,
Sucked in by breath,
Absorbed through flesh,
Sent rushing in my bloodstream
To refresh and sustain what allows our union,
To aerate and conquer what destroys our intercourse.

I awaken to your precious self
As I sense the hot breath of a lover,
The tiny, fragile breath of a baby held,
The contented, rumbling purr of a pet.

I awaken to your precious self
When I smell aromas of flavors or flowers,
When you caress me as the treetops,
When I'm denied the purity of your love.

You are my omnipresent lover,
I take you for granted
As I take you;
I walk through you and past you
Without thanksgiving.

You yourself never harm me.
But the soil of my abuse of you
Clings to your life-giving atoms,
Causing me to sputter and cough,
Threatening the very life you give me.

Forgive me,
Forgive us.
But thank you.

Move me,
Ocean depths within,
Ebb and flow
With feeling.

The tide is out
And I'm bereft.
The tide is in
And I overflow.

Ah-hah!
Ah-yes!
Ah-love!
Prescience,
Purpose,
Passion—
Full.

You surge within my body,
I feel your flow,
I feel.
You drain out of my body,
I feel you go,
I feel.

Oh-no!
Loveless,
Useless,
Thoughtless—
Spent.

Fill me,
Fill me full,
Fulfill me,
O holy water:
troubled,
still,
living,
moving.

Fill me,
Move me,
Flow through me.

Your glow draws me,
Draws me in, draws me out,
Whether in heart or hearth,
Mind or machine,
Great soul or big sky.

I feel you on me,
I feel you in me,
Uniting as igniting,
Burning out barriers,
Soldering as one.

I run when you're too passionate,
All-consuming, suffocating.
I rest when you're self-contained,
All-embracing, invigorating.

Whether or not you get me quickly,
Ultimately, you will have me:
I will join the slow cremation
Of degenerating earth
And be recycled in other life.

But of the glow that's me uniquely,
What becomes?
Does it feed the glow of others?
Does it return as yet another?
Does it enter a joyful, cosmic bonfire?
Does it join itself to God?
Or do I fade and disappear?

I may not have a choice,
But I do have the choice to hope.
Hope is a fire that burns from here to there,
Faith is the glow that believes in "there,"
Love is the spark of choice.

*T*angible,

Sensual,

Here and now,

Are you more than you seem?

Atoms,

Patterns,

Systems—

Is there a plan?

With your siblings

Water, fire, air,

Are you all there are

Setting us in motion?

Or are you craft,

Creation, creature

Of something invisible,

Some first "umph"?

As we,

Are you product

Of a twinkle in the eye,

A seduction of the flesh,

An orgasm of delight,

Of gestation and labor,

A painful, slimy birth,

Of sucking at a breast,

Of growth toward awareness?

The ancients have said so.

Are we too smart for visions

Or too taken with our own dreams

That we no longer look back,

Behind, beneath, beyond

Our simple explanations

To a grander dream and Dreamer?

Do we fail to quest for truth

In our search for fact?

Do we overlook fertile soil

In our desire for bedrock?

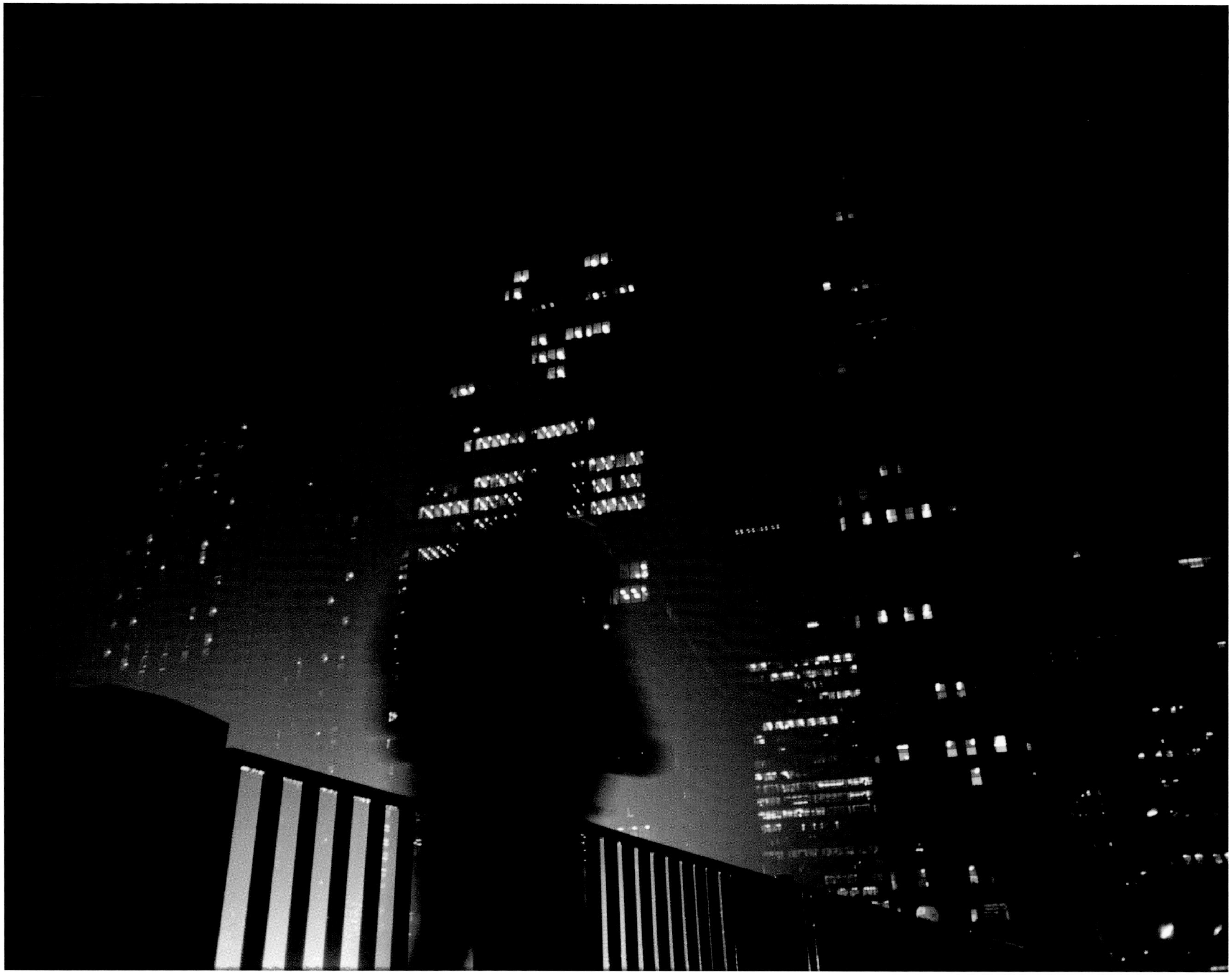

Slow, shallow breath of sleep,
Rapid breath of action,
Rhythmic breath of running,
Gasp for breath in panic,
Paced breath of meditation,
Burst of breath in climax—

Echoes of first breath
When cast ashore
Out of milky ways:
The stars, the sea, the womb.

The urge to breathe:
Whose? Mine alone?
Or was I taught
In genes, in complicated codes
Fired into inert mud
By design?

Who or what first breathed
Into earth and water and fire
The breath of air, of life?
Was it the will of Earth, Air, Water, Fire,
A natural, unstoppable conspiracy?
A Will so powerful we proclaim it
Adonai, Allah, Brahma, Great Spirit;
A Will so inscrutable we frame it as
Art, literature, religion, science;
A Will so wild we tame it by
Dance, dreams, muse, myth?

Breathing has evolved
Those who wonder.

Pulled into the air,
Gathered into bundles,
Pushed along the sky,
Released from on high,
Spilling your guts on earth,
Sinking underground,
Cascading along the surface,
Channeled into gaps of earth,
Wedged between the continents,
Pulled to and fro.

What moves you?
We ask. We explain.
How. What. Where. When. Why.
But yet, we wonder.

Your beauty,
Your terror,
Your fecundity.

Your cycle spawns life.
Whose labor delivered you?
A battle of the gods?
A heavenly courtship?
A divine word spoken over chaos?
A sensory illusion of Maya?
A cosmic sleight of hand?
A collective unconscious dream?
A primordial explosion?

Full of wonder, the possibilities.
Full of wonder, we.

Echoes of Prometheus
In the voices of zealots,
Patriots, revolutionaries, reformers,
Evangelists, visionaries, marketeers, coaches, teachers,
Taking the forbidden fruit
Of fire from the gods,
Igniting our souls
With passions and visions and energy
So we may be like gods
In our appetites and accomplishments.

Yet our appetites and accomplishments
Are mere emanations of sacred fire,
Cast in shadow by eternal light
Consumed by apocalyptic flames:
Something greater than us is here.

Do we bow to you, O sun and stars?
To you, dark space?
Or do your own light and shadows reveal
Something greater still?—
A cosmic shadow box
For some higher power,
Some greater light,
An immortal truth,
An essence,
An aroma
Savored as it burns?

We burn with wonder.

You were formed,
You form us,
Now we form you.

We strip you,
Tunnel you,
Level you,
Grade you,
Bind you.

We graze you,
Farm you,
Mine you,
Build on you,
Build in you.

We mold you,
Fire you,
Glaze you,
Paint you,
Gaze at you.

We explore you,
Preserve you,
Defend you,
Hold you,
Tend you.

We are you,
Make love to you,
Pray for you,
Reflect on you,
Return to you.

We reform you,
You reform us,
You are refreshed.
Hallelujah!

CYCLE NINE

You are permeated:
Sound waves,
Radio waves,
Light waves,
Micro waves.

We ride these waves
With conversation and music,
With recordings and radar,
With cinema and laser,
With television and radio,
With communication and cooking.

You are gracious,
Allowing these waves to live and move
And have their way in you.

Teach us your grace,
Opening our selves to veiled waves
Of spirit and divinity.

May we welcome these waves
With gratitude and growth,
With meditation and mindfulness,
With compassion and care,
With prayer and praise.
With love and hope.

May we be gracious,
Allowing sacred waves
To have their way in us.

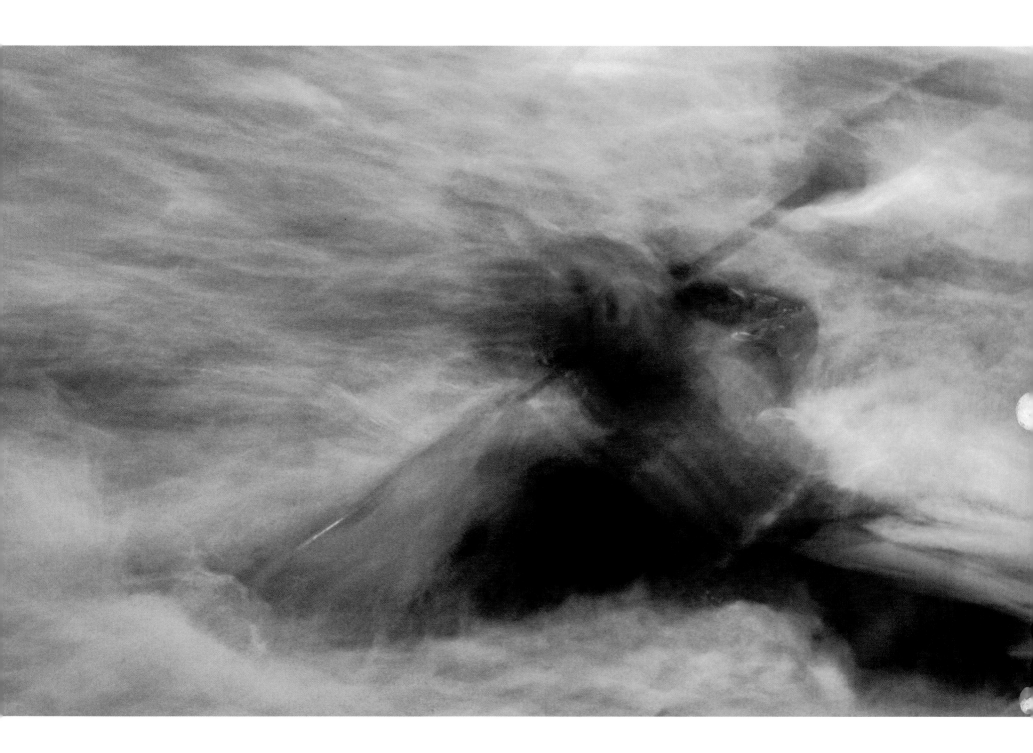

You ou insist on being close to me.

Though I cover myself—
You pound from above,
Determined to drench me;
Slip in casually and intimately
As I enter you for a swim;
Seep out my pores
As I go about my daily tasks;
Swim around my eyes
In the privacy of deepest feeling;
Fill up my inmost self
Seeking release through a hidden channel.

When I uncover myself,
Your pounding shower awakens me,
Your gentle smooth pools pleasure me,
Your humid breath refreshes me,
Your moist torrent releases me,
Your setting free relaxes me.

Jealous of air's embrace,
Of earth's hold on me,
Of fire's exclusionary flames—
You try to displace air,
To submerge earth,
To douse flames.

You once held me in my mother's womb,
You were the womb of all living things,
You sacrificed yourself on earth's burning altars
So we may live.

Now I hold you within my earth,
Breathing into you my breath,
Warming you with my flame,
And you live.

Water,
I am your child.
Water,
I am your reservoir.

We measure you.
We use you.
We buy you.
We sell you.
You are our servant,
A commodity—
Yet your home is the heavens.

We fear you.
We bind you.
We bury you.
We send you back to heaven.
You are our nightmare,
A horrific image of absolute evil
Torturing lost souls.

Yet you have a soul
Emancipated from regulation,
You have a sacred self
That burns chaff from seed
And smelts iron from ore.

Incensually arousing our sensuality
We dance around your light as one—
Glow of the heavens on earth, in earth,
Candle, campfire, sacrificial conflagration:
Cremate our folly, cauterize our wounds,
Galvanize our intentions and gusto for life.

We throw ourselves into the flames
And yet are not consumed:
We are of the fire, but not in the fire.
There we meet our origin and our end,
Spark of divinity.

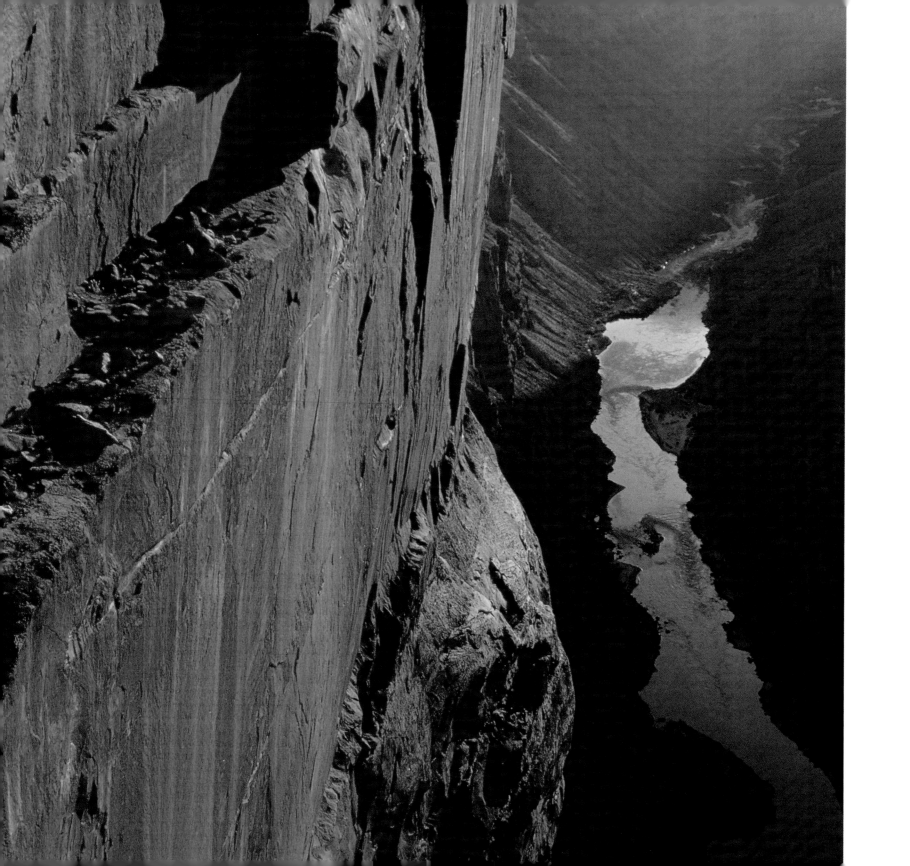

*H*ow we love to straighten you out,
Wash you off, dump on you,
Look down on you,
Cover you up.

Water moves with your curves,
Gets dirty with you, cleanses you,
Dives deep into you,
Uncovers your majesty.

Air whistles around your crevices,
Mixes with your sand, dusts you off,
Carries you up to heaven,
Tears at all that cloaks you.

Fire explodes your smooth surface into mountains,
Melts your elements together, refines you,
Looks up to you from your core,
Experiences you inside and out.

Your friends must teach us to mingle with you!
To enjoy nooks and crannies,
To get down and dirty,
To restore your purity,
To look down to you,
To look up to you,
To let you breathe.

May we dream of earth
As much as the heavens.

Earth is in heaven.

s a mighty wind
You swept over chaos
Before it was organized.

You wrestled with earth,
You struggled with water,
You battled with fire.

You kissed them
With your breath:
Life called from inertia.

We behold you in awe.

As a mighty wind
You sweep over order
And create chaos.

You wrestle with earth,
You struggle with water,
You battle with fire.

You crush life
With your breath:
And return all to chaos.

We behold you in fear.

Thou givest, and
Thou takest away.

As a mighty wind
Spirit sweeps through order and chaos alike,
By both, creating our human community:

Awed by life, assuaging fear,
Offering gratitude and grief,
Perspective and expectation.

We behold it in awe.

We give, and
We receive.

Burning,

Parched,

Thirsty,

Empty,

Dusty,

Dry,

Wizened,

Faint,

Listless,

Shrunken,

Shriveled,

Senseless,

Death.

Fall,

Rinse,

Flush,

Cleanse,

Replenish,

Renew,

Restore,

Grow,

Nurture,

Swell,

Blossom,

Pleasure,

Quench.

Tides of the heart,

Streams of the mind,

Surges of the body,

Cure droughts of Soul.

Transform me.
Burn fat,
Ignite muscle,
Cauterize wounds,
Consume chaff,
Smelt essence,
Anneal strengths.

My revolution!
Out of the flames
Of my former world
I move forward,
Ashes falling aside,
Lean, solid, focused,
Open, reaching, ready,
Clear, concise, capable.

My reformation!
Out of the womb
Of my former self
I move onward:
A new creature
Fired, fired up, fired off,
Breathing, absorbing,
Receiving and welcoming.

My resurrection!
Out of the tomb
Of dead dreams
And dreams of death,
I move!
Alive, fluid, dancing,
Whirling, singing, praising,
Thankful and celebrative.

Transform me!
Lighten, strengthen, heal,
Purify, rarefy, temper—
O sacred blaze within!

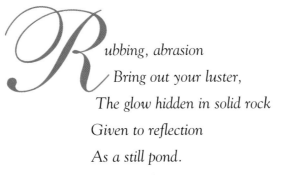

*R*ubbing, abrasion
  Bring out your luster,
    The glow hidden in solid rock
Given to reflection
As a still pond.

Pleasure, adversity
Bring out our shine,
Revealing an unknown flare
Given to resurrection
Out of our depths.

CYCLE ELEVEN

So accommodating,
So open—
You receive all guests:
Friend, fiend,
Feathery, furry,
Fuming, filmy,
Flowery, fruity,
Funky, fetid—
All with equanimity.

You need your friends—
Earth, to block unwanted company,
Water, to flush out your house,
Fire, to cremate the dead.

Thank you, friends,
For discernment,
For cleansing,
For elimination.

You pound,
 You caress,
You push,
You tickle,
You gush all at once,
You trickle one drop at a time,
Invited or uninvited,
Welcome or unwelcome,
With or without warning,
You offend or delight,
You destroy or lift up,
You drown or you float,
You terrify or you amaze,
You pacify or you entertain—
Thanks to your acolytes:
Earth, for focus,
Air, for freedom,
Fire, for transformation.

You have been the center of our dance.

From bonfires ablaze to candles flickering,

Wildly we have swung around you,

Howling, shouting, singing, chanting,

Igniting our passion for uniting

For war, for the hunt, for community, for the gods.

We treat you like dirt.
Yet you are the center of all we know,
All we touch, all we see, all we taste,
All we smell, all we hear, all we feel.
Unaware, we are completely attentive to you.
We ignore our absolute dependence on you.
We behave as if you cannot know us in return,
Cannot touch, see, or taste us,
Cannot smell, hear, and feel us—
Regarded as an idol masquerading as a god.

Yet you give us this day our daily bread.
You give us your kingdom.
You make up the substance of all
That touches, sees, tastes, smells, hears, feels, and knows us.
Without you,
We would be unknown, unloved, and unremembered.
You are God incarnate,
And the very soul of you is what we worship
As if it were far removed
When it is far within.

CYCLE TWELVE

I dream sometimes of flying,
Naked, through your winds,
And I cannot help but think
That I belong in you.

It must be that the part of me
Which is yourself, the air—
Hopes for a reunion
Up there.

I nod, and I dip in flight,
I lift my head, and rise,
The soaring lifts my soul
And I know myself as free.

I was meant to fly—
Not knowing what this means—
But it feels natural and delightful
And I feel released.

I sometimes dream of flying:
My bare skin wrapped within your arms;
Borne aloft by your hidden strength,
My hand reaches up beyond my grasp.

Orgasm rediscovers that hidden spring
Where life was first conceived
And thus celebrates
Life's anniversary
With pleasure.

Orgasm releases that hidden spring
Surrounded by the Garden
Where sacred and naked flesh
Communed
In innocence.

Orgasm remembers that hidden spring
Where earth, air, water, fire danced
To make a thing
Aspire
To life.

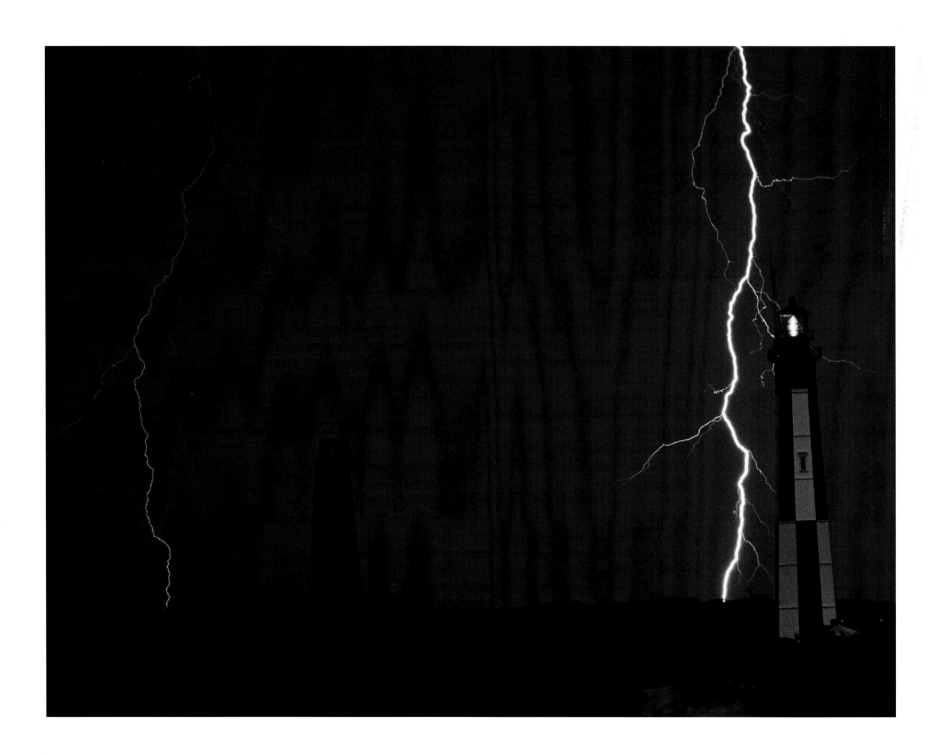

Galaxies glimmer,
  Then they're gone.
Even the heavens
Give way to dawn.

Flashes of lightning
Quick disappear;
Only then their voices
Touch the ear.

Glowing faces
Fade into memory;
The hearth of the heart
Thus never quite empty.